IF YOU WERE A KID AT THE
SIGNING OF THE CONSTITUTION

BY JANEL RODRÍGUEZ · ILLUSTRATED BY MAKENZIE MCCARTHY

CHILDREN'S PRESS®

An Imprint of Scholastic Inc.

Special thanks to our consultant, Dr. Le'Trice Donaldson, assistant professor of history at Auburn University, for making sure the nonfiction text of this book is authentic and historically accurate.

NOTE TO THE READER, PARENT, LIBRARIAN, AND TEACHER: This book combines a historical fiction narrative with nonfiction fact boxes. While all the nonfiction fact boxes are historically accurate and true, the fiction comes solely from the imaginations of the author and illustrator. The author and the editors acknowledge that, during this same time period, the experience of kids from races, ethnicities, and/or backgrounds other than the ones featured was extremely different.

Library of Congress Cataloging-in-Publication Data available

ISBN 978-1-5461-3619-4 (library binding) / ISBN 978-1-5461-3620-0 (paperback)

10 9 8 7 6 5 4 3 2 1   25 26 27 28 29

Printed in China 62
First edition, 2025

Book design by Kathleen Petelinsek

Photos ©: 9: Look and Learn/Bridgeman Images; 11: John Greim/LightRocket/Getty Images; 13: Shutterstock; 15: Wally Gobetz/Flickr; 21: Library of Congress; 23: giftlegacy/Getty Images; 25: VCG Wilson/Corbis/Getty Images; 27: Michael Ventura/Alamy Images.

All other photos © Shutterstock.

TABLE OF CONTENTS

A Different Way of Life

The summer of 1787 was an important time in American history. Back then, the United States was about 10 years old and made up of only 13 states. It was a young country in need of law and order. To address this, **delegates** from 12 of the 13 states gathered in Philadelphia, in the state of Pennsylvania, to create the **Constitution**. This very important **document** would establish the government and outline how the nation would be run.

Imagine life in the United States around that time. States like Pennsylvania and New York were mainly made up of farms. Children often worked with their parents instead of going to school. There were no highways, railroads, or telephones. There was no president.

Turn the page to travel to the early years of the United States. You will see that life today is different from how it was in the past.

Meet Elisabeth!

Elisabeth Norris lives with her grandfather, the caretaker of Philadelphia's famous Pennsylvania State House. She helps him oversee the grounds and keep the building and its meeting rooms clean. But her work has become harder ever since the state delegates have been gathering there. Newspapermen, British soldiers, and others have been sneaking around, trying to spy on the private meetings inside.

Meet Archie!

Archie Walters lives nearby, in a room above the City Tavern. It's an inn and restaurant that his family owns. Like Elisabeth and many other children, he doesn't go to school. Instead, he helps his family by working at the inn. He serves food and drinks, does odd jobs, runs errands, and makes deliveries. This has made him a familiar face to people around town.

Archie carefully tucked corn bread and bottled drinks inside of two pails.

"Tell Mr. Franklin I'll have boiled apples ready for him tonight," the cook said. "You know they're his favorite."

"Okay!" Archie wiped sweat off his forehead, picked up the pails, and set off for the Pennsylvania State House. All summer long he had delivered food to the leaders meeting there. Many of them also ate at the City Tavern after their meetings.

CREATING THE LAW OF THE LAND

We call the 55 state leaders who together outlined the new government the "framers of the Constitution." Their meeting is known as the Constitutional Convention. They gathered in Philadelphia after traveling from 12 different states. Because there were no cars, highways, or airplanes, it took a long time to travel from one place to another. People often took boats up or down the Atlantic coastline to travel between the states. Elderly Benjamin Franklin, who lived in town, was the exception. He traveled to the meetings by sedan chair.

This is what a typical sedan chair looked like. It moved thanks to manpower—not horsepower!

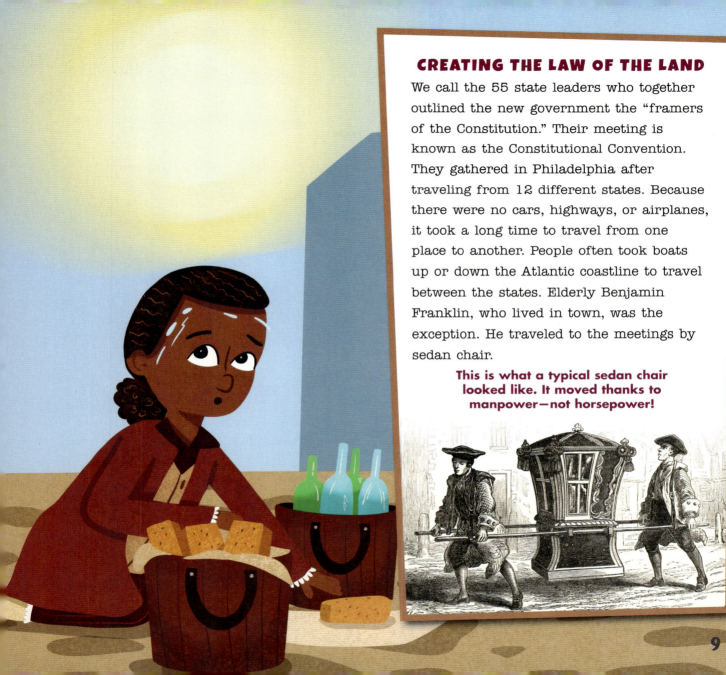

Elisabeth looked out the clock tower window and watched as a boy approached. She often stood there, watching the grounds for anyone sneaking around the meeting hall. She'd seen the boy make deliveries often. But he'd never noticed her before.

Then, to her surprise, he looked up, caught sight of her, and dropped his buckets. Ducking out of sight, she flattened herself against a wall and thought, *I must be more careful!*

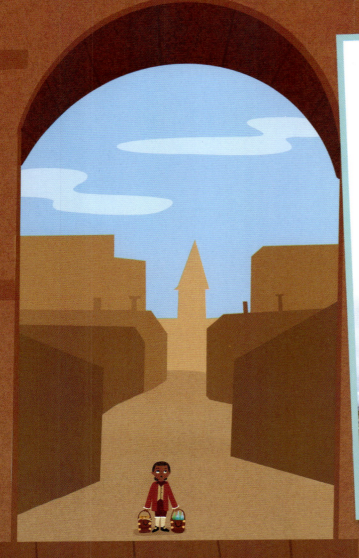

A NATIONAL LANDMARK

Pennsylvania State House is now known as Independence Hall. Because of its important role in U.S. history, it is the most popular tourist attraction in Philadelphia. It was where both the Declaration of Independence and the Constitution were debated and signed. It was also where the first two presidents of the United States, George Washington and John Adams, were sworn in.

This is Independence Hall. It was the home of the U.S. government from 1790 to 1800.

Archie picked up the buckets he had
dropped. There had been someone in
the bell tower watching him. He thought
it was a young girl at first. But then she
disappeared, and a haunting sound filled
the air. "*Wooooooo! Wooooooo!*"

She must be a ghost! Archie thought. He
ran toward the men guarding the meeting
room doors. Hadn't they heard that?

One of the men stepped in front of him.
"Stop," he said, raising his hand.

KEEP OUT

In the beginning, the delegates came together to fix a document called the Articles of Confederation, an agreement between the states that had been adopted in 1777. But it soon became clear that a true constitution was needed. So the delegates decided to create something new—but keep it secret. They did not want newspapers sharing anything about their meetings until they were done.

This is the actual room where the Constitution was signed.

"We'll take those," one guard said as another looked inside the pails. "Shoo!"

They opened the door. A blast of warm, sticky air and a few buzzing flies escaped from the room.

Though there were many people inside, Archie was still able to quickly find a familiar face. "I have a message for Mr. Franklin!" he said.

"Is that young Archie?" a voice called out. "Let him in!"

THINGS GET HEATED

The delegates kept all the windows and doors of the state house shut for privacy. Unfortunately, this also kept in the summer heat. And there were no T-shirts or shorts back then. Men wore long sleeves, vests, jackets—even wigs! Sweating through long meetings six days a week made the delegates cranky. Maybe this contributed to them breaking into heated arguments!

The room was packed, which added to the heat.

Elisabeth took another look out the window. Was that someone hiding behind a tree? The guards were too busy with the boy to notice! Elisabeth quickly ran downstairs, hoping to alert the guards before it was too late.

On her way outside, she peeked inside the meeting room. The boy was there, talking to Mr. Franklin. "Let us return to order," a voice boomed. As the men took their seats, the boy turned and saw her looking at him.

FAMOUS FACES

The delegates were all men. Women were not allowed to be public leaders then. Today, we still remember some of the delegates by name—George Washington, Benjamin Franklin, Alexander Hamilton—because they played big roles in founding the country. James Madison is called the "Father of the Constitution" because he wrote so much of it.

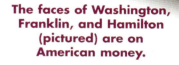

The faces of Washington, Franklin, and Hamilton (pictured) are on American money.

Elisabeth waved the boy over.

Archie joined her behind the door. "Are you a ghost?" he asked.

"No." She smiled.

"Then, who are you?" he asked.

Elisabeth pointed out a nearby window. "Look!"

Archie saw a man creeping along the bushes nearby. "Who is that?"

"Someone must be trying to spy on the meeting," Elisabeth explained. "We have to stop him!"

Archie opened the window to yell.

"Wait," Elisabeth said. "I have a special signal."

HOT TOPICS

One argument the framers did not want the public to know about concerned slavery. Some delegates wanted it outlawed in the Constitution. But others did not. They refused to sign the Constitution until the others backed down. Slavery wasn't banned until many decades later, in 1865, when the 13th Amendment to the Constitution was passed.

President Abraham Lincoln signed the document that officially banned slavery in the United States. Today, the Lincoln Memorial in Washington, D.C., honors his legacy.

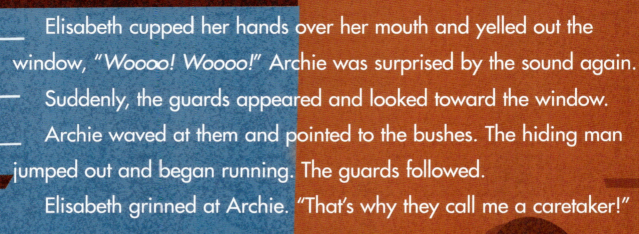

Elisabeth cupped her hands over her mouth and yelled out the window, "Woooo! Woooo!" Archie was surprised by the sound again.

Suddenly, the guards appeared and looked toward the window.

Archie waved at them and pointed to the bushes. The hiding man jumped out and began running. The guards followed.

Elisabeth grinned at Archie. "That's why they call me a caretaker!"

Archie laughed. "Well, you certainly 'took care' of him!"

Then, the sound of a banging gavel made them both jump.

STATE VS. FEDERAL GOVERNMENT

Another major decision the delegates made was whether each state should run its own government or if one national government should run them all. In the end, they chose both. The federal, or national, government would manage the military, collect some taxes, and print money. Separate state governments would handle other matters within each state.

The United States motto, *E pluribus unum*, means "Out of many, one."

Elisabeth and Archie peeked inside the meeting room.

A tall, gray-haired man stood in the front.

"That's General George Washington," Archie said. "I met him earlier in the summer."

Washington picked up four sheets of parchment and began to speak. "We the people of the United States, in order to form a more perfect union . . ."

Elisabeth looked at Archie. "This must be what they've been working on!"

WRITER AND SCRIBE

James Madison (who later became the fourth president of the United States) took the decisions the delegates had made about the new government and used them to write the Constitution. After that, the document itself was handwritten by Jacob Shallus, who was paid to copy Madison's words neatly and clearly.

Shallus was paid $30 for his work. That is more than $1,000 in today's money.

When he was done, General Washington called the men to vote. "Those in favor of making this the Constitution of the United States, say 'aye.'"

"Aye!" Voices rang out.

Cheers could be heard around the room.

Washington smiled. "Now come forward and sign your name."

Archie closed the door. "What was that all about?"

Elisabeth shook her head. "I think this means…that they are finally done with their meetings!"

CHECKS AND BALANCES

The Constitution established three branches of the U.S. government. The **legislative** branch (Congress) is made up of elected **representatives** from each state. It creates new laws. The **executive** branch—the president and his cabinet of advisors—leads the country by carrying out those laws. Finally, the **judicial** branch is made up of courts of judges that protect the Constitution. Each branch holds powers the others don't. No one branch has full control over the government. This way the branches can keep each other in check and balance each other out.

George Washington was voted the president of the Constitutional Convention.

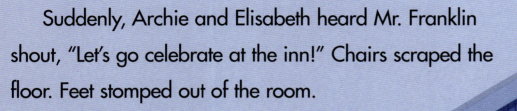

Suddenly, Archie and Elisabeth heard Mr. Franklin shout, "Let's go celebrate at the inn!" Chairs scraped the floor. Feet stomped out of the room.

When the kids finally opened the door again, there was no one there.

"I should go help," Archie said. "But can I come back later? I'll bring you some boiled apples to celebrate."

Elisabeth smiled. "Celebrate that we're a real country now?"

"And…" Archie laughed. "That you're not a ghost!"

A LIVING DOCUMENT

After it was signed, the U.S. Constitution had to be ratified, or officially approved, by state governments. Later, 10 amendments outlining the rights of every citizen were added (the Bill of Rights). Since then, 17 more amendments have passed, stating major changes to the way the country is run, and making the Constitution even stronger.

The original Constitution is kept at the National Archives Museum in Washington, D.C.

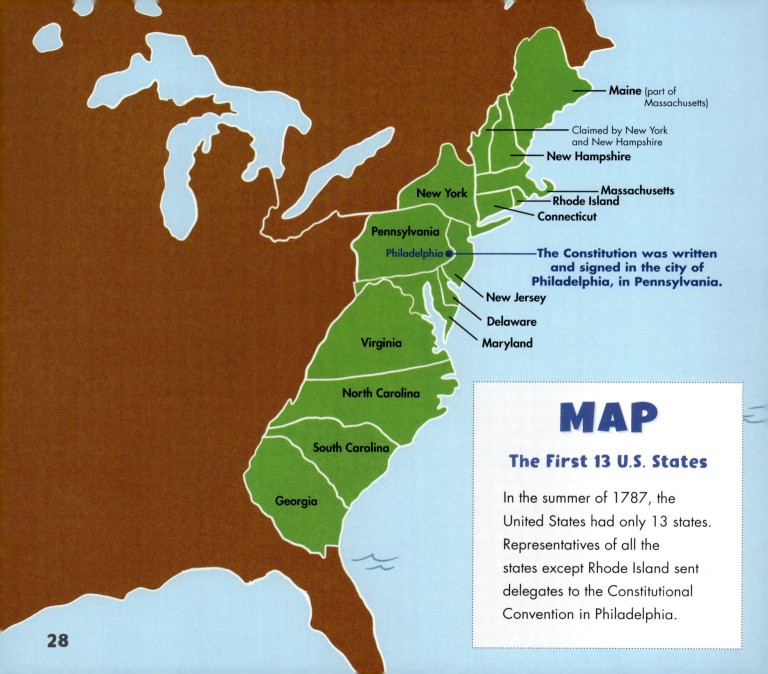

Maine (part of Massachusetts)

Claimed by New York and New Hampshire

New Hampshire

New York

Massachusetts

Rhode Island

Connecticut

Pennsylvania

Philadelphia ●

The Constitution was written and signed in the city of Philadelphia, in Pennsylvania.

New Jersey

Delaware

Maryland

Virginia

North Carolina

South Carolina

Georgia

MAP

The First 13 U.S. States

In the summer of 1787, the United States had only 13 states. Representatives of all the states except Rhode Island sent delegates to the Constitutional Convention in Philadelphia.

TIMELINE

May 25, 1787 The Constitutional Convention has enough delegates to officially begin.

September 17, 1787 The Constitutional Convention ends with the signing of the Constitution after almost four months of closed-door meetings.

March 9, 1789 The U.S. government starts to officially operate under the Constitution.

December 15, 1791 The first 10 amendments—together, called the Bill of Rights— are added to the Constitution.

January 31, 1865 The 13th Amendment is passed, banning slavery.

June 4, 1919 The 19th Amendment is passed, giving women the right to vote.

Today The Constitution is still "the highest law of the land."

WORDS TO KNOW

constitution (kahn-sti-TOO-shuhn) the basic laws of a country that state the rights of the people and the powers of the government

delegates (DEL-i-gitz) people who represent other people at a meeting or in a legislature

document (DAHK-yuh-muhnt) a piece of paper containing official information

executive (ig-ZEK-yuh-tiv) of or having to do with the branch of government that carries out the laws of the United States or any state

judicial (joo-DISH-uhl) of or having to do with a court of law or a judge, as in *the judicial system*

legislative (LEJ-is-lay-tiv) of or having to do with the process of making or changing laws

representatives (rep-ri-ZEN-tuh-tivz) people who are chosen to speak or act for others